FOCUS: How iFOCUS4Life Mastery

Module#2 – HIT THE MARK!
IT
Strategies to Catapulting Visionaries
& Entrepreneurs to Great Success

John W Rhodes

MASTERY

Table of Contents

Copy Chart & Join the

iF4LM 30 Day Challenge

iFOCUS4Life Mastery 30 Day Challenge

On __/__/__ I ______________ accept ______________ Challenge

	Mon	Tues	Wed	Thur	Fri	Sat	Sun
Key Principles/ Weeks	i	F	O	C	U	S	Review Principles
Week 1							
Week 2							
Week 3							
Week 4							
iF4L MasteryWk.							
Total							

(iF4L Daily Challenge Chart)

Module#2 – HIT THE MARK! IT

Ifocus4Life Mastery Module 2

1st Become Laser Focus

This book reveals how to be accurate in achieving results of monumental goals, plans, and purpose with biblical proportions. With the goals and plans you make, there must be a focus and not just ordinary focus, but the right one. You don't want to spend your time and effort focusing on something, and then later realize you were focused on the wrong thing.

Therefore, it is crucial at this stage of the game while you read this book to make sure that you:

#1 – Seek God first concerning your goals and plans in order to maximize your efforts, time and money, and ensure they are not wasted.

#2 – Have a primary focus.

#3 – Must have the right focus.

#4 – Follow a process to reach your goals.

#5 – Be persistent & focused daily towards reaching your goal.

#6 – Focus on what you are able or capable to focus on.

#7 – Have determination, vigilance and a fighting spirit.

#8 – Take on the right amount of focus you can handle.

#9 – Become laser focused to flush out the chatter, distraction, clutter, etc.

#10 – Understand that what you focus on should be of overall and long term betterment to those you serve, and not just yourself.

#11 – Know the end result of your focus should be for God's glory, not yours, no matter what your goals are.

#12 – Ask yourself this question; if and when you reach your goals and complete your plans, will God get the glory? Does God get the glory?

This book aims at helping you gain results that are great and mighty as you are dependent upon the Lord's help. It's about helping you go beyond the norm to walking in the supernatural, practical ways.

"Helping Lives Keep Their Faith

Flowing through every Cell & Heart of Life

for Abundant, Fulfilling & Purposeful Living."

AJWR

"You Must Aim Above to Hit the Mark"

– John W Rhodes –

You may have heard the quote by Ralph Waldo Emerson which says, "You must aim above the mark to hit the mark." However, I say to you with a spiritual emphasis to "aim above to hit the mark." When you aim above, your sights are focused on God and His purposes for your life; in fact, you call on the wisdom and understanding from above to help you execute the plans of God.

First of all, let me say that you must set in your heart to hit the mark! Nothing is too hard for our God. He plants the ideas and desires in our hearts, and should the desire in your heart truly be of God, believe that it is not too hard for God to perform.

"Ah, Lord GOD! Behold, thou hast made the heaven and the earth by thy great power and stretched out arm, and there is nothing too hard for thee: [18] Thou shewest lovingkindness unto thousands, and recompenses the iniquity of the fathers into the bosom of their children after them: the Great, the Mighty God, the LORD of hosts, is His name..." Jeremiah 32:17-18.

Here, the other great thing about this is that God is known as The Great & The Mighty God, in which I will expound upon a little later in this chapter.

We aim to touch the heart of God through worship, prayer, and His Word. In all we do, we must seek God first if we want Him to show us great things beyond the norm.

Motto Text 1:

"Thus saith the Lord the maker thereof,
the Lord that formed it, to establish it; the Lord is
his name; 3 Call unto me, and I will answer thee,
and show thee great and mighty things, which thou
knowest not." Jeremiah 33:2-3

"You may show me a man of talent, but I'd rather
see a man of talent and wisdom. For I know he uses
his for the glory of God."

John W Rhodes

THE LORD

The Lord means someone or something having power, authority, or influence; a master or ruler.

If we desire to be effective in hitting the mark in the endeavors we embark upon, we must allow our Lord and Ruler to rule over us and show us exactly what He wants to do with our life. And peradventure we are doing something that is not in His will, rest assured, He will redirect us and show us exactly what must be done or how to do what has been placed in our heart. God is the Master orchestrator, and He knows how to make music with and in our lives. Therefore, let the Master Conductor perform His great and mighty work in you and you will be a joy for the world to listen to – your life played out on the different instruments of life.

Let God have total power and authority over our lives so that we can master the gifts that have been planted within us.

It is at this point of total surrender to His Lordship that we can see Mastery being developed in all that we do in life.

THE MAKER

Maker means, 1. A person or thing that makes or produces something. 2. God; the Creator.

We understand by this definition that a maker is one who produces something. To produce means to make or manufacture from components or raw materials (Webster). Therefore, our maker has a purpose and a plan to produce certain results in our lives. He can take nothing, raw talent, and the bare necessities and make it into something great and mighty. What we have to do is simply trust the process for He is forming us into His master plan and perfect handy work. Just as the Potter with the Clay, He knows exactly how to fashion it for His use.

As you are making plans, allow the maker to guide, lead and direct you while using His wisdom, knowledge, and understanding; then you will be more effective than you could ever be.

IT

What is your "IT"

Whatever "It" is that you have purposed in your heart or that which God has planted in your heart, it is imperative that you seek the will of God first for "its" purpose.

The Lord is our maker and the maker of everything in our lives; don't you think He knows what's best for what He has given you? Often, I reflect upon the fact that God gave me the gift and talent of playing the trumpet. I have put it down (stopped playing), and then picked it up (again). People would ask me to play, then I would feel inspired to play a song off the cuff, or write and create a new song. Eventually, I came to the realization that this is a gift, and it isn't going anywhere. Do I get a little rusty? Yes, but I pick "it" (trumpet) up again and start playing or practicing. One of the most joyous experience is to play my trumpet during special occasions; by request at my workplace and along with Kevin, my co-worker, who plays bass, and he's truly a blessing to play alongside, not to mention that music has bonded our work relationship – music creates a universal language that everyone can relate to and get involved in. We have had some great times and sessions with co-workers. Here again, is an example that the gift of music and talent with the trumpet are not my own. It all belongs to God. I simply need to be available to be used by Him when He speaks.

Expression of thoughts has become my gift when it comes to writing words down, and the writing of books has become a talent. So, my expressions in writing are God's gift to me. The books I have produced are just an extension of those thoughts placed in either articles or books to help bless others in the Mark-It. Those I HIT THE MARK! It, I do so using my gift to reach those whom God wants to speak to through expressions of my thoughts, which come from ABOVE.

Remember again that the Lord is the maker of all that I have, therefore, I must ask the creator how, when, where, and for what purpose should I use what He has given me to be most effective in the Hitting the Mark-It.

In case you have not grasped or noticed it yet, there is a play of the words Mark! It. These words are of threefold. "Mark" is the target or task in which we aim to execute effectively, "It" is the gift or talent you have been given by God to reach a God-ordained purpose, and "Mark! It" stands for Marketplace; where that gift will be used in the market to meet a given need. Merriam-Webster defines a marketplace as:

1. a: Marketplace is an open square or place in a town where markets or public sales are held.

b: market; the marketplace is the interpreter of supply and demand. 2: the world of trade or economic activity: the everyday world.

This is why calling upon the Lord is imperative so that you can use your gift for its intended calling or purpose.

FORMED IT

It is the Lord who is the maker of all things and formed it.

"Thus saith the Lord the maker thereof, the Lord that formed it..." Jeremiah 33:2

The word formed comes from the root word "form" which according to Webster's dictionary means, "bring together parts or combine to create (something)."

Therefore, in a physical sense, God had an intended purpose for the thing that was created to be developed into. When we begin or pick up a new talent or new skill, we initially don't know what the new skill or talent will be developed into; but after some time, and with practice and study, we begin to see some results. And if we are persistent and diligent at developing "It," we begin to notice that "It" is now taking form, and the results for which it was created in a physical sense are now taking place. Still, what is so amazing is that sometimes we don't know its ultimate purpose until days, weeks, months or even years down the line. However, God knew what "It" would be used for and who would be used as an instrument to bring forth its purpose. Now, even though I am saying it,

14

which applies to the new skill, thing or talent developed, God knew you and your purpose on earth even before you were created or formed in your mother's womb. Therefore, when we tap into knowing the Master's will for our lives, everything that we touch will come to life with progressive improvement. Therefore, the more we spend time with the creator who created us and who gave us the creation in which we are developing, the more effective we will be in using "it" for its original and intended purpose. The key here is to stay connected as we progress, and the Master will help us perfect what it is we that have, even through challenges, difficulties and time.

"Then the word of the Lord came unto me, saying, 5 before I formed thee in the belly I knew thee; and before thou camest forth out of the womb, I sanctified thee, and I ordained thee a prophet unto the nations." Jeremiah 1:4-5.

ESTABLISH IT

"Thus saith the Lord the maker thereof, the Lord that formed it, to establish it…" Jeremiah 33:2

Now, once you have mastered the thing "It" which was given to you, the next order of business is to "Establish It" & "Yourself" in your field of study. For example, a dentist goes to school to get a degree in that particular field, but even after the degree, a certain level of practical study must occur, rather as an apprentice. Once that occurs and they pass the test, they may desire to open their own dentistry. Once they set up their dentistry and go through the necessary paperwork, it is at that moment that they become established.

The word established means having been in existence for a long time and therefore recognized and generally accepted.

It also means a church or religion recognized by the government as the national church or religion.

The LORD is His Name.

The Lord himself reminds us that it is He who has created us and has formed us for His use. Thus, the important thing is to follow His ways while drawing close to Him for He knows exactly what we need. In addition, God knows everything that has been created and knows its best use and the times and seasons when it's most effective.

So,

Write the words spoken to you in a book

"The word that came to Jeremiah from the Lord, saying,

2 Thus speaketh the Lord God of Israel, saying, Write thee all the words that I have spoken unto thee in a book.

3 For, lo, the days come, saith the Lord, that I will bring again the captivity of my people Israel and Judah, saith the Lord: and I will cause them to return to the land that I gave to their fathers, and they shall possess it." Jeremiah 30:1-3.

Before I will deal with the six iF4LM key principles of executing plans God's way, I want to share with you five characteristics of a focused disciple of Christ that must be taken into consideration before and while making your plans in several areas of your life.

The characteristics are as follows:

1. Integrity

2. Discipline

3. Positioning

4. Leadership

5. Kingdom-Driven

Consider these elements as precursors before executing your plan God's way. These elements will be within each focus key. Look for them directly or indirectly to help you determine if your personal plans are in alignment with God's way of doing things. Understand that these are not a means to an end, but are to be used as tools to help you focus while re-building your life, building your legacy or simply desiring to establish habits of success in your daily life.

Integrity Principle

Integrity (making sure your heart is right before your plans take flight). What is your personal agenda? Be honest with yourself and to those whom you will speak to or influence.

Integrity means strict adherence to a standard of value or conduct; personal honesty and independence, completeness: unity, soundness (Webster's).

"When a man's ways please the Lord, he maketh even his enemies to be at peace with him." Proverbs 16:7.

Two great benefits of walking in integrity are that your enemies will be at peace with you even when they don't want to. The second benefit is that the Spirit of the Lord shall lift a standard against them. That standard is Victory for God's chosen ones; it is making reference to Jehovah-Nissi, the Lord our banner, who gives us victory.

The presence of the Lord shall be with you as you make plans and carry them out. You don't have any other choice but to succeed when the Lord's presence is with you.

Discipline

Discipline is making sure you put in the necessary work, preparation, plans, precision, etc.

Discipline according to the dictionary of Bible themes is defined as "Loving and corrective training that leads to maturity and responsibility on the part of those who experience it."

Discipline is training intended to elicit (to bring out or call out) a specified pattern of behavior or character, behavior that results from such training. ***A condition of order based on obedience to authority.

"If you are faithful in little things, you will be faithful in large ones. But if you are dishonest in little things, you won't be honest with greater responsibilities." Luke 16:10.

This is also true of the story of the Talents (Matthew 25:14-30). He who had the greater talents was faithful in little, thus the Lord gave him more. The additional talents came from that which the one who had one was unfaithful and slothful to use, and thus his gifts were taken from him due to his lack of self-discipline. The word discipleship comes from discipline. Therefore, if we desire to walk as Christ did and be an example of Christ, we must be disciplined in the things that God has entrusted to us here on earth, and not just the so-called spiritual things.

Positioning

Positioning (are you where God wants you to be in that given moment of challenges, mandate, trials, and pre-elevation?) The word said to Jehoshaphat after careful preparation and before the initial battle was "You will not need to fight in this battle. Position yourselves, stand still and see the salvation of the Lord, who is with you, O Judah and Jerusalem! Do not fear nor be dismayed; tomorrow go out against them, for the Lord is with you." II Chronicles 20:17.

Position is the place or location occupied by something; its right or proper place. It is a bodily posture or sitting position, relative place or situation. A viewpoint: an attitude. A post of employment: a job. Social status or official rank. The place in a proper position. (Webster's)

Leadership

Leadership is the action of leading a group of people or an organization. (Google)

It is the activity of leading a group of people or an organization, or the ability to do this. Leadership involves establishing a clear vision, sharing that vision with others so that they will follow willingly, and providing the information, knowledge, and methods to realize that vision. (Business Dictionary)

What I love about the first definition is that it says leadership is the "action" of leading a group of people. One must take action if he or she intends to truly lead a group of people and not be afraid of making mistakes or offending someone. Brian Tracy, one of the world leading authorities on business and personal development says, "The key to success is to focus our conscious mind on things we desire, not on the things we fear."

Listen, I am the first to tell you that there are small or big decisions I have made in the past that were wrong, off centered, and wasn't the best judgment, though at that time it seemed to be. However, I had to make a decision and I led the people in the direction I believed was best for all. This simply says that leadership is being willing to make a decision, and even when you are not totally sure of what the outcome would be, you hope and make plans for the best.

You must be courageous, creative, compassionate, and humble when taking a position of leadership, but first, leadership starts in the mind and the belief that you can lead others and do it effectively with God's help.

The key to successful leadership is obeying God, rather than man while making decisions.

"Obedience is better than sacrifice."

Now that you have a general basis to the type of characteristics needed to be a successful disciple, let us look at the six Ifocus4Life principles in executing daily plans for your life and the kingdom.

This brings us to the next characteristic – Kingdom-Driven.

When we speak of being Kingdom-Driven, it involves more than the immediate circumference or territory that you are in. A kingdom encompasses a broad and expanded territory.

Jabez grasped this vision in his heart and asked God for help to expand and to enlarge his territory (I Chronicles 4:9&10). One of the questions I have for you is, are you thinking too small or have you asked God to expand your territory? If so, how much expansion of your territory are you seeing? Lastly, are you making the plans to expand the immediate vision you have been given to a greater or global vision? Are you thinking, "Biggie Smalls" as one of my fellow clergy said once on a FB post, "As you are in a smaller place right now, prepare yourself for what is ahead by perfecting your gift now, and becoming as skilled and trained as you can for the greater next level." (Paraphrase words said by Lucrecia Booker Weathers)

Jabez prayed a prayer that we can copy on a frequent basis,

"And Jabez was more honorable than his brethren: and his mother called his name Jabez, saying

because I bare him with sorrow. And Jabez called on the God of Israel, saying, Oh that thou wouldest bless me indeed, and enlarge my coast, and that thine hand might be with me, and that thou wouldest keep me from evil, that it may not grieve me! And God granted him that which he requested." I Chronicles 4:9-10.

1. First, he called on God

2. He asked God to bless him undeniably

3. He asked God to enlarge his coast or territory

4. Asked that God's Hand would be with him.

5. Keep him from evil.

6. As a result of his prayer, God granted him his request.

I believe that when Jabez called on the God of Israel and asked Him to expand his territory, he was thinking of the needs of others he could help and bless and not just himself. In other words, Jabez was not being selfish or just church minded; Jabez was being Kingdom-Minded because he wanted to help meet the needs of the kingdom and not just help his immediate need. This leads me to our last characteristics of a focused disciple of Christ, which is Kingdom-Driven.

Kingdom-Driven

KD is the ability to look beyond your immediate needs and see the needs of not only others but the needs of the masses. When you think like this, your life will forever be changed. This is why having a business plan or a vision in place is critical to the overall development of your dreams, promise, and vision. Jesus was being Kingdom-Driven when He saw the need of the five thousand who needed to be fed when He fed them with the five loaves of bread and the two fish according to Mark 6:41.

I learned over the past weekend that Kingdom Building is about praying and preparing the next generation to take the lead and to do it by example. Kingdom Building is about seeing what needs to be done and making preparation in getting it done, while never making excuses but just doing it – just like Nehemiah saw that the wall was broken down and he made the necessary preparations through prayer and preparation of planning to get it done.

Read Nehemiah Chapter 4:13-14. We will talk more about this in our iF4L Key Principles.

IFOCUS4Life Mastery Keys & Principles

I- Initiate – Gen. 1:1-5

F- Follow up – Luke 18:1-7, 11:5-13

O- Organized – 1 Cor.14:33, 40, Gen.1:4

C-Consistent – Luke 11:5-13

U-Unity – 1 Cor. 13:1-13, Luke 11:17

S-Strategy – Proverbs 24:6-7, Joshua 6, I Chron.12:32

FOCUS KEY#1

I - INITIATE

iF4LM Motto Text: I – Gen.1:1-5

The word 'initiate' means to begin or to cause something to begin. It also means to cause to begin: start or launch. To introduce someone to a new interest or activity. (Webster's)

The first valuable aspect before executing any plan is to make the choice to Decide. To decide means to settle, to conclude, and to make up one's mind. Once you have made up your mind, there is no turning back. The song that comes to my mind is, "my mind's made up; no turning back," I believe, by the late Milton Brunson. Also, the more current song, I won't go back, by William McDowell.

God has placed witty inventions within us. We are not to let those inventions lay dormant, we are to showcase them to the world. As a business owner or a worship leader, an artist or an engineer, we are responsible for the level of skilled training we acquire to introduce what God has shown to us, to reveal it to the world and not be afraid. One of the best ways to do anything is to take the liberty to initiate the task. Before the "task" is begun, the most critical step is to pray first.

Worship – Pray – Decision – Preparation – Work

Start the process with prayer and set out to win. Don't wait for someone else; you initiate the action to make a change or difference in the world, in your environment or life.

Secondly, decide. To decide means,

1. To choose something, especially after thinking carefully about several possibilities. In other words, "Go ahead and make up your mind and do it."

Commit and then do it.

Practical iF4LM Tip #1

PLAN. To plan is very important if you desire to carry out anything.

Plan out your next day the night before. This simple task may seem very easy and at times manual, however, it has the potential to increase your productivity twice over (10x).

Never underestimate the power of a well thought out plan and action.

Practical iF4LM Tip #2

Set an Alarm Account for the Set Time.

[14] Is anything too hard for the LORD? At the time appointed I will return unto thee, according to the time of life, and Sarah shall have a son. Genesis 18:14.

I have found out that one of the easiest ways to do anything is by using a clock/stopwatch on your phone; then start. Decide and then do it. Just Do It! As Nike's motto says. What hinders people from doing the things they should do? Is it fear? If it is fear, remember that "God has not given us the spirit of fear, but of power, love and a sound mind." II Timothy 1:7. We covered this in Module One, so I won't spend much time on this. However, when there are times we seem unable to get going and need a jump start, set a time to do the task and do it.

To break the cycle of procrastination, I use the law of 21/7, which is what the Holy Spirit gave me. I had heard that if you do something consistently for 21 days, it becomes a habit. Well, I broke that down into further detail by choosing to do something for 7 minutes to start with. I would first decide to do the task for 7 minutes, pick a time to do it, get out my stopwatch app on my cell phone, set it for 7 minutes, then start. Even if I didn't go beyond the seven minutes, the whole point was to start. Often, once I started, I would do the task two more times which is equivalent to 21 minutes.

For example, I wanted to break the procrastination cycle of not practicing my trumpet by beginning to practice my trumpet on a regular basis, two to three times per week, for 21 minutes each session to start with. While I would choose to do this in the late hour, about 9 pm or 10 pm, here again, was an example of me putting off till the last hour of the day so to speak; however, I did do it. Once I did the first 7 minutes, the second 7 minutes became easier, and before I knew it, I was practicing for about an hour.

Do what I call the 7 minutes POP-UP! exercise.

Prompt Obedience Produces a Unified Purpose.

This is similar to POP! UP! Shops. You choose a place (not the normal set up) for an extended amount of time, and you provide the service.

In this instance, you put into action immediately the "most resistant, reluctant, or feared task" you have been putting off. Go ahead and start now. I am.

List   what   you   did?

_____

How   much   time   did   you   do   it   for?

_____

How long ago has it been since you did that task?

_____

How do you feel now that you have done the 7minutes   POP!   UP!   Exercise?

_____
_____
_____
_____.

Now that you have done 7minutes of a reluctant or put off task, I challenge you to the 7 days of P.E. No, this is not Physical Education although it requires physical or mental exertion.

These 7 days of P.E. includes a plan, then execution of that planned task. Here is how it goes, you take 7minutes to pray and receive instruction & or strength about the task. Take 7minutes to plan your task, then 7minutes more to do the task for a total of 21minutes. Do this for 7 days straight. Once you have mastered the 7 days, take the challenge further and go seven more days, then after that, one more set of seven days and it will be an equivalent of 21 days.

Practical iF4LM Tip #3

Don't Procrastinate: Take Action.

Don't procrastinate, especially when you know what you need to do. There are times when we are afraid and not sure about some things, and we start examining something and analyzing it over and over again. This is what some call the analysis of paralysis. This is where we analyze something so much that we do nothing at all. If you have prayed about something, have the knowledge on how to do it, the skill is set, and most of all, you've got the ok in your spirit from the Holy Spirit, then move forward. You won't ever learn if you don't move ahead and take action. Faith without works is dead.

Practical iF4LM Tip #4

Provide New Ideas.

We are waiting for new ideas and unless you provide new ideas to those who need them, they won't be helped. You see that what you have in you is not only for you. So get over it! Get over yourself and do what is necessary to help others. You may say, "I don't want to do something unprepared, or if I do anything, I want to present it with excellence." You can, but you must begin somewhere. Don't be afraid of making mistakes or afraid of the critique someone else will give you. Just do it! How else will you know if what you have will make a difference in someone else's life unless you create, make, and present the idea? However, it is going to take initiation on your part to make a difference. Regardless of what area of expertise you have or gifts you possess, if you don't use them, they aren't any good to anyone, not even to yourself, because you are not using them. If you need to activate the gift inside of you, then do so by declaring and decreeing that you shall do what God has called you to do. For example, you know God has called you to be a teacher, then make preparations to go to school or attend classes. Declare that "you will find the resources, obtain the grades to get a scholarship, that the loans or grants you need to go to school will be available for you in the Name of Jesus." God has given us a mandate and assigned a specific task over our lives, but we must first acknowledge the responsibility assigned to us and move forward.

Acknowledge Your Called Responsibility.

The first step to going forward is to acknowledge what God has called you to do and then do it. We acknowledge that God created the whole world and that without Him there would be nothing. Upon knowing that, we also have rest in knowing that because God made us in His image, we are to follow His example when it comes to creating things.

Practical iF4LM Tip#5

Prioritize What You Need to Do.

Being gifted has its good and bad, especially when you know how to balance and use what you have. This is where prioritizing what you have been given to do is necessary. You can't possibly do everything all at once. If you try to do several things at once, you are only stressing yourself then you end up frustrated because you are not accomplishing anything. I recall when I recently had to shut down many business endeavors because I was just wasting both money and time. So, I shut down my credit cards in which monthly authorships were taken out of my business account, and I was not making progress with the tools that cost me the monthly authorships. Needless to say, I was being a good steward over God's money. Even though I was using my so-called pocket change to feed into my business, it was still being wasted simply because I wasn't using business systems that cost me monthly. I started out trying to learn several new business systems all at once only to be frustrated because one, I didn't stick with one long enough to learn it effectively, and once I learned the business system tool, I didn't have enough time to apply it, which again was another waste. Long story short, once I shut down the credit cards, it was such a relief because I was able to narrow my business system tools down to one or two at a time in order to master and produce results.

When it comes to having dominion and creating things, projects, task, and ideas, it should be second nature to us, after all, that's what God created us to do and to be – little creators. Think about it, everything you see, God created it, and at the same time, God used man to initiate the idea of bringing it into existence. The reason you are able to read this is because someone created a computer program and a computer so that ideas could be created and placed on a word file like Microsoft Word, which again, was created by a man, Bill Gates. God gave him an idea, but he took the idea and advanced it.

Before you create the "What," you must first ask WHY? Why are you creating what you are doing or providing? Secondly, who will benefit from it?

I'm sure Bill Gates, the Wright Brothers, Dr. George Washington Carver all asked that question, "why am I doing or creating this thing?"

The book, "The Effective Executive" by Peter F. Drucker, says "The effective executive focuses on contribution. He looks up from his work outwards toward goals." He asks: "What can I contribute that will significantly affect the performance and the results of the institution I serve?" His emphasis is on responsibility. The focus on contribution is the key to effectiveness: in a man's own work – its content, its level, its standards, and its impacts; in the relationship with others…"

When I read this, it brought back to my mind the need to pay attention to my intentions and see if what I am doing is for the betterment of mankind, in making effective positive changes.

The next question you must ask yourself is "who or what specific group of people am I creating this thing or creating service for?"

What have you created that is useful to others?

What is your vision that you are casting? Here is a question you must ask yourself whether it is a new business or a new ministry or church.

1. Can it be duplicated?

2. Can it be done without me in the picture?

3. Can it be enlarged or expanded? We say enlarge my territory, but is your territory and vision expandable with what you are equipped with?

4. What preparations have you put into the vision or task at hand? Do you just wish and hope that God comes in to bless the mess, or bless your stress because you lacked the discipline to prepare not only the external components to get it done, but failed to prepare the inner man to deal with the challenges present before or ahead of you?

5. Can it grow beyond you? How much? How far?

6. You are reading this lesson because God placed the idea within me to share it with you so you can learn greater ways and strategies on how to focus more in life in order to bring Him glory. So I ask you, how have you taken the initiative to take your God-given role to another level of creativity? Whether you are a mother, wife, husband, laborer, manager, teacher, social worker, pastor, lawyer, doctor, business owner, etc., are you using your God-given creativity, and not just your authority to help others in order that the Kingdom of God is advanced? "The kingdom of heaven suffereth violence and the violent take it by force." – Matthew 11:12. Some things must take a great amount of effort to move forward; restraint isn't needed when advancement is calling your name. Meaning you will have to suffer some things which may include the use of time, money, talent, creativity, resources for the good of the bigger picture.

"In the beginning, God created the heavens and the earth..." Genesis 1:1. What are you creating, or are you waiting for that perfect moment to come by, when life will pass you by, then you will look up and say, "Where did time go, or what happened to the desire of my heart, whereby I didn't do the things I always wanted to do, because time got away from me or I didn't have the money or resources to expand the current vision?" We can make up all the excuses in the world, but what will matter is at the end, will God say, well done my good and faithful servant or will He say, depart from me ye worker of iniquity because we wasted both His time, money, resources and the ability to create. (Matthew 25:23, 7:23).

The entertainment world compensates those who use their creativity. I wonder why? Not really, I know they appreciate the creativity of those who go beyond the norm of themselves in order to create a vision or paint a picture or an idea that expands the mind. If the world compensates its own, how much more will God compensate you for creating ideas for the Kingdom of God. Our reward expands far beyond the natural and temporal into the spiritual and eternal.

What things or actions have you personally initiated to make your life, relations, home, ministry, work, health, and mind better? Let's talk about it. (Take this moment before going into the following questions).

Write down three things you initiated this week or today and share it with the group; be as brief as possible; one minute per person.

"To Scale Higher, You Must Dig Deeper and to Stand Longer; your Foundation must be Solid." – John W Rhodes

This was a true reality that hit me hard when I was planning to take my "hobby" marketing business to a serious realm. I say hobby because that's how I was treating it. First thing I failed to do properly was set in motion my business plan. It is considered a "plan in motion." Until I put it together, thought it out thoroughly and followed it to the "T," I couldn't call it a true business; and yes I was registered with the city, but still I lacked two major components that were keeping my business B.E.E.M. from taking off, and that was first a Solid Business Plan and persistent discipline to carry it out. I needed a major paradigm shift from **"Winging it, to Wining It."** A concept I had to develop to remind and ask myself, which one am I doing? So, what transformed my business from a hobby to a full-scale profitable business was when I set my mind to complete the **"Business Plan and Work the Plan as I Envisioned It."** We want the fruits of prosperity, but don't want to put in the discipline to reap the benefits.

Here are simple questions to include in your business plan before you start? By the way, this goes for non-profits or churches/ ministries.

1. What is your market?

2. What is the major problem you're attacking?

3. How are you planning to solve that problem?

4. How will you continue to provide a solution to the problem?

Brendon Burchard from High-Performance Academy says, *"When you knock on the door of opportunity, do not be surprised that it is Work who answers."*

When you initiate a task or an idea, expect work to follow it, which includes again discipline to get it done efficiently.

I leave with you at the end of this focus key a quote by Maya Angelou on facing challenges,

"You will face many defeats in your life, but never let yourself be defeated."

TAKING Q.A.R.E. OF BUSINESS SECTION:

KEY#1 – INITIATE

QUESTIONS – APPLICATION – REFLECTION – EXCEL'LE'RATION

I -Initiate – Gen.1:1-5

Q.A.R & E:

Q's:

What did God do in the beginning? _____

What should we be doing as Believers in our everyday lives? _____.

When there is nothing in existence what do we do? _____,

What did God do? _____.

A'S:

Once you see that it is good, what do you do?
_____.

After bringing order to it, what should you do with
it? _____.

What can you do on a daily basis in this area?
_____.

R'S:

What do you personally believe should be involved
in initiating action?

When do you have the most trouble *initiating action*
even after you know what to do?
_____ and in what area mostly?
_____

E'S:

How can you Excel-le-Rate this Key Principle in
your life?

    a. What would it take for you to operate with the
spirit of excellence?

    b. Rate yourself on the scale of one to ten. How
do you initiate action? (One being less, ten
being very pro-active).

c. What will it take for you to accelerate this FOCUS KEY#1 initiate action in every area of your life?

d. On the scale of one to ten, how do you rate yourself as an action taker?

_____

e. Now how do you rate yourself in taking action doing the right thing at the right time?

_____

Word of Wisdom: **Many people are doing a lot of things, but are they doing the right things at the right time. And are they called out to do those things?**

M&M: Gen.1:1-5

1 In the beginning, God created the heavens and the earth. ²Now the earth was formless and empty, darkness was over the surface of the deep, and the Spirit of God was hovering over the waters.

³And God said, "Let there be light," and there was light. ⁴God saw that the light was good, and he separated the light from the darkness. ⁵God

called the light "day," and the darkness he called "night." And there was evening, and there was morning—the first day.

FOCUS KEY#2

F - FOLLOW UP

iF4LM Motto Text: Luke 18:1-7, 11:5-13

In the world of business, It is said: "fortune is in the follow-up." That means that if you follow up the potential customer, they will eventually respond with paying you for your goods or services, which will lead to wealth. During my years of network marketing and small business endeavors, I held true to this saying and saw the blessings manifest before my eyes that the fortune truly was in the follow-up. However, that follow-up was not without constant effort, diligence, hard work, sweat, tears, and rejection at times.

The phrase "follow-up" means the act of repeating or supplementing the previous action, as by a letter, or visit. In today's world, that follow-up can also come through instant messaging on social network platforms such as Facebook, Twitter, Instagram, Snapchat, and of course email, text, or good old fashion telephone call.

Our prayers are to have the same pursuit as that businessman or woman who will not quit until they get what they ask for.

In Luke 18:1, it says, And he spake a parable unto them to this end, that men ought always to pray, and not to faint; 2Saying, There was in a city a judge, which feared not God, neither regarded man: 3And there was a widow in that city; and she came unto him, saying, Avenge me of mine adversary. 4And he would not for a while: but afterwards, he said within himself, though I fear not God, nor regard man; 5Yet because this widow troubleth me, I will avenge her, lest by her continual coming she weary me. 6And the Lord said, Hear what the unjust judge saith.

Men are to always pray and not to faint. Though you may find yourself in a difficult situation, the easy thing would be to stop praying and give up in defeat, standing in denial and doubt saying maybe it is God's will not to pursue the matter any further. How many times have you found yourself doubting what the Holy Spirit told you He would do, but because it had not happened at the time you thought it should happen, you gave up and said to yourself, well, I guess it wasn't the Lord's will. You must have the tenacious pursuit like the widow who troubled the unjust judge until she got what she wanted. Hold fast to your faith and don't allow the enemy to steal that which God gave to you. If you have prepared yourself properly with what He gave you, then go forward, and don't stop until you get it.

Imagine having a need throughout the whole day such as food, and you have no money, but you know a friend whom you could ask for help. The friend says he's too busy right now, but you continue to ask him, then finally at midnight, he responds simply because you kept asking. Is your midnight hour right around the corner, will you stop at 11:55 pm, short of your blessing? We must be like the persistent friend when asking Jesus to move on our behalf. Some people say, if you keep asking then you don't believe, which isn't true. If that was the case, then Jesus would never have used the following parable about asking, seeking and knocking.

In Luke 11:5-10. 5 And he said unto them, Which of you shall have a friend, and shall go unto him at midnight, and say unto him, Friend, lend me three loaves;

6 For a friend of mine in his journey to come to me, and I have nothing to set before him?

7 And he from within shall answer and say, Trouble me not: the door is now shut, and my children are with me in bed; I cannot rise and give thee.

8 I say unto you, though he will not rise and give him, because he is his friend, yet because of his importunity he will rise and give him as many as he needeth.

9 And I say unto you, Ask, and it shall be given you; seek, and ye shall find; knock, and it shall be opened unto you.

10 For every one that asketh receiveth; and he that seeketh findeth, and to him that knocketh it shall be opened.

Three simple, yet profound steps to your breakthrough to answered prayer are as follows:

First, ask for what you desire in the will of God.

Asking is a process in which we have formulated a question in our mind to inquire about, to request, or invite or demand, a need, desire, a want, or an explanation.

Secondly, seek out the answer and resource, and how your prayer can be answered to what you desire.

Thirdly, keep knocking at the door of opportunity even when it seems like what you are praying for is not going to happen.

TAKING Q.A.R.E. OF BUSINESS SECTION:

KEY#2 - Follow Up

QUESTIONS – APPLICATION – REFLECTION –EXCEL'LE'RATION

F – Follow Up: Luke 18:1-7, 11:5-13

Q.A.R & E:

Q's:

The _____ is in the _____up

When should men pray? _____.

If we pray_____ what will not happen? _____.

What was the widow trying to do to her adversary _____ what did she keep doing till she got an answer _____.

What did the unjust judge do_____ & why? _____.

A's:

Are there some things you have been asking God to do, but because it hasn't happened you begin to doubt and wonder if it will come to pass? _____.

If so, how can you defend your faith and go forward despite   the   opposition?
_____

_____.

R's:

A.S.K. should involve

A stands for _____   **S** stands for _____   **K** stands for

_____

 What   does   it   truly   mean   to   A.S.K.?
_____

_____

When should we expect to see the results after we A.S.K.?_____

_____.

E's:

How can we pray with excellence while making sure we follow up with our initial prayer request?
_____

How can we increase our acceleration & momentum when   it   comes   to   praying?
_____.

48

On the Scale of One to Ten, one being the least and ten being greatest, how persistent are you in following up on your prayer request made to God?

_____

Let's pray: that we walk more like Christ in all we do even in our productivity and creation here on earth.

Let's pray: for persistence until we see results.

M&M: Luke 18:5-7 [5] Yet because this widow troubleth me, I will avenge her, lest by her continual coming she weary me.

[6] And the Lord said, Hear what the unjust judge saith. [7] And shall not God avenge his own elect,

which cries day and night unto him, though he bears long with them?

FOCUS KEY#*3* – ORGANIZED

iF4LM Motto Text: 1 Cor.14:33, 40, Gen.1:4, Hab.2:2

4 And God saw the light, that it was good: and God divided the light from the darkness. Gen.1:4

OPERATE WITH PEACE IN MIND

"For God is not the author of confusion, but of peace, as in all churches of the saints." – I Cor.14:33.

"Let all things be done decently and in order." V.40

Having peace in your presence is an indication that there is order in your midst. I have found out over the years that even in a work environment, if there is no clear and concise order of how things should be, confusion and disorder will arise. Having the wrong people in charge will cause disorder and serious problems in your organization. You may try to make it work or even try to force it to work, but each time, you will come up with confusion, chaos and ultimately, disorder. Here is where the wisdom of God comes in and even the gift of knowledge. Favoritism must not be chosen over character, ability, and commitment. Just because we have been friends with someone over the years, even that they have been in your work department or even in your community, should not dictate or validate placing them in the power of authority or higher position. If this is done without careful consideration of other factors, it can cause possible disruption in your organization. Sometimes people are likable but don't have the adequate amount of skill level to perform the job. They may even have experience but not the type of skill level of experience needed to execute the job. Then on the order hand, they may have the skill set, but lack the ability to get along with others, thus putting them in a high level or supervisory position will only cause more disruption to your organization in the long run.

THE STAND

One thing that is very important in our walk is learning how to balance things out in our lives and organize our lives in a way that doesn't cause what we call, "burn-out." There are times we fight in fights that we have no business fighting in. Maybe it's a concern or certain plans that don't involve us directly; this only 'zaps' our strength, time and focus.

You find that God "saw that the light was good, and He then divided it." The revelation here is that when God saw that the light was good, He separated it from the dark. Putting things into categories is one of the keys to keeping your strength. Knowing when to rise in the morning and when to go to bed is simple, but how many of us at times overextend ourselves then we wonder why we are so tired. This is why God created a day and a night time. Also, learn to be a part of positive things or be around positive people. Stand and be part of groups or developments that build people up and not tear them down. Why be a part of something that will cause you heartache and pain in the long run? Have you ever heard the saying, "I don't have a bark in the fight?" Why be a part of something that is of wrong standing, or whereby someone or organization is bringing harm upon others or yourself, yet you still support it? When we are present where there is dysfunction, corruption, animosity, and division, we are part of the big picture – unless God wants you in a particular place to be an example and to also help to make a change.

It is hard to separate yourself from a group of people you love, especially family and church folks. Ultimately, you know what's really good for you in the long run, and you sometimes have to make some tough decisions. It's not being merciless, but real in your perception and stand on what's going on, and what you see.

God sometimes uses us to bring order to a thing or situation that needs to be corrected even when we are abused or mistreated. When God's people are mistreated, that is the time He expects us to stand up for ourselves and watch Him move on our behalf. Just like Joseph who had jealous brothers, and God still used the whole situation of Joseph's trials to prove that he went through persecution in order to bring those who persecuted him out of future potential death and starvation. Joseph's situation was providential to the betterment of mankind. What are you passionate about? Start making preparations to bring that vision into existence or to take it to another level.

THE PLAN

God is a God of order. He is the Master who brings to order what is out of line and what needs adjustments in one's vision. Again, God saw that the light was good. God has given us a vision. The question is do we recognize what is in front of us as being good or bad? Once we do, what steps have we taken to make it right or to perfect what we already have? Our disposition to matters of life has a direct correlation to how successful we are. Writing down what we desire to do is one way of staying organized. The question is: "Will we or are we writing down the plans that God has for us to do daily? When we "do it off the cuff," we do God a dis-service (does He not deserves more?) I'm not saying we should not be flexible in the things of God, but what I am saying is that if we don't take time to prepare for things concerning the Kingdom of God and our personal lives, we will end up frustrated and wonder why our lives are in such disarray. We make decisions due to the lack of prayer and due to not writing down what we are really feeling. I have learned most recently that if I am having a serious disagreement, I put it in writing, be it at work, church, or home, in order to make things a lot clearer. If you are anything like me, sometimes I need several reminders to execute important tasks, not because I'm lazy or I'm not paying attention, but because I get busy. If I don't do it right then, I will soon forget. For example, my wife will ask me to do some handyman chores or simple chores around the house, and of course, because I don't see them as urgent, what do I do? I say, ok I will do it later. Well, later doesn't come fast enough or it's much later than what I said. I know no one else is like that, right? That's ok, God is working on me. Anyway, I will say to her, "Honey, can you write that down for me?" Ladies and gentlemen, you probably know her reply, like many other women, "Why do I have to write it down? I have already told you several times." (Laughing). Anyway, when my wife writes it down for me and puts it on the refrigerator, it becomes front and center; it's not out of sight, out of mind. Eventually, I do it, because I remember to check my "Honey's To-Do List." Have you ever heard the saying, "if you fail to plan, you plan to fail." It's true. You must take the time to write out the things you plan to do, then take action. My recent learning about time management and planning is to schedule the time I plan on doing something and stick to it.

Habakkuk 2 says, "To write the vision and to make it plain."

We must take this scripture very seriously if we plan on doing some serious business for the kingdom of God.

The enemy plans and schemes against us; yes, even in writing. So how much more should we write and plan how we are going to overthrow Satan's kingdom?

…"And God saw"… We are to stand upon our "watch and see." We are watching to see what God will say to us. Are we watching and planning what next move we need to make for His Kingdom? Am I doing it according to what God has instructed me to do for my family, my marriage, my job, my health, my business, my community, my education, city, etc.?"

WRITE IT DOWN

"Where there is no vision, the people perish: but he that keepeth the law, happy is he." Proverb 29:18.

Notice it says, "Happy is he that keeps the law. How do we know what God's law is? Yes, the law. Well, "it is written." The laws of the land are even written, of course, just in case someone breaks the law; they will be reminded of that same law.

Here's another strategy given by God "… divided the light from the darkness." If we learn to divide our task into little manageable steps or task, we can do all that we are ordained to do. If something is difficult to do, set a timer for 5minutes and start. Of course, it may take you more time to do the task, however, the aim is to start, and most often once you get started, the time will increase as you set your timer again. Why is this so important? The answer is because the enemy or we ourselves allow the stealing of our time from God. Not only have we allowed our time to be stolen from each other, our spouses, etc., but even our time with our children has been stolen! We must give them a sufficient amount of time, nurturing and teaching them. We can't just say, "not now," or "because mommy or daddy says so." If we don't create a balance with our children with school, extra-curricular activities, worship, fellowship, then we have kids growing up feeling bitter about their parents or even about the church, school, etc.

A healthy balance must be created so that healthy people are developed for the Kingdom.

Once you have **the idea**, you **stand on it**, **plan it**, **write it**, then the next step is to **carry it out**. This involves **taking action**, but also getting the like-minded people or groups who are also willing to help support what you are doing. Being highly organized is not only putting things together but also carrying things forward to make a change, or to make a difference.

We often hear that faith without works is dead. This it is true. You can talk about what you want to do or what you want to become, or talk about taking action to change things, but unless you put action behind what you believe in and be willing to move forward with your plans, it's all "hot air." What happens to a hot air balloon? It goes up, but once the air gets out, the balloon comes down.

KEY#3 – ORGANIZED

QUESTIONS – APPLICATION –
REFLECTION –EXCEL'LE'RATION

O -Organized – 1 Cor.14:33, 40, Gen.1:4

Q.A.R & E:

Q's:

1. When something is in disorder, what should you do?   &   why?

_____

_____

2. How can you tell when something is not of God according   to v.33_____.

3. What is the result of being organized?

_____

A's:

4. How must all things be done?

_____

a. Why? _____

5. What did God do that was an example of being organized? _____

6. What are the three major ways you can be organized? _____.

7. How can you accelerate your goals for growth? _____.

R'S:

8. How can you move with a Spirit of excellence? _____.

9. One scale of 1 to 10, how organized are you at home_____, at work_____, or in your business _____.

E's

10. Does your daily organization or disorganization reflect in the progression of what you do? _____

11. Why? Or why not? _____.

M&M's: 1 Cor.14:33, 40

"For God is not the author of confusion, but of peace, as in all churches of the saints." I Cor.14:33

"Let all things be done decently and in order." V.40

FOCUS KEY#4

CONSISTENT

We must not give up when opposition comes your way.

If4LM Motto Text: C- Consistent - Luke 11:5-13

Consistent means: agreeing or accordant; constantly adhering to the same principles

Opposition comes at those times when our character is being developed, or when lessons must be learned in order to grow. We must not "be weary in well doing, for in due season…" Galatians 6:9. Ask yourself, what season are you in and are you willing to pursue the things of God no matter the cost? It may not be easy, but God will give you the strength to get it done if you have the <u>desire,</u> <u>will,</u> and <u>discipline</u> to do it! We asked God for the almost "unseemly dreams" to come to pass in our lives, but we have to be persistent in asking God for each step of direction in the process. If we don't put in the time or acquire the discipline, and hard work that is required, then we may start to become angry at God when things don't come to pass. Are you in a season of preparation? Then, prepare wisely and with tenacity; watch God move as you stay in His will. There is a quote that talks about how persistence can be more than talent.

"Nothing in this world can take the place of persistence. Talent will not; nothing is more common than unsuccessful men with talent. Genius will not; unrewarded genius is almost a proverb. Education will not; the world is full of educated derelicts. Persistence and determination alone are omnipotent. The slogan "Press On!" has solved and always will solve the problems of the human race." – Calvin Coolidge

If God has given you a vision, then ask for direction. If you are gifted, but yet confused about where, when and how to use your gift, don't cry about it, just ask God, seek direction and start knocking. 8 I say unto you, "though he will not rise and give him, because he is his friend. Yet because of his ___persistence,___ He will rise and give him as many as he needeth."

9 And I say unto you, Ask, and it shall be given you; seek, and ye shall find; knock, and it shall be opened unto you.

10 For every one that asketh receiveth; and he that seeketh findeth, and to him that knocketh it shall be opened. (Luke 11:8-10).

When things are not going your way, don't give up, start knocking on heaven's gates. God will answer you. He may want you to choose a different direction or to go about what you desire in a different way. Just don't make excuses as to why you can't do something; find, meditate and pray about a way to get it done. "Get Her Done, in Jesus Name."

I remember when I was having a difficult time in college and didn't know if I could even make it through another semester; my Aunt told me the story of "the Tortoise and the Hare." This story spoke volumes and placed hope in my life. She reiterated that story to me several times and used the following scripture to re-enforce it, "The race is not given to the swift nor to the strong but to them that endure to the end." Ecclesiastes 9:11.

We have to draw a line in the sand and stand. We have to make up our minds by faith. Are we going to go back to where we came from or are we going to move forward no matter the cost? Especially, if we know that God has a great plan in store for us in the direction we are currently going. This current path may not seem comfortable, but I know from personal experience that "if God brought you to it, He will certainly take you through it." What you are going through is to build character and to make you stronger for what is ahead.

So, keep asking, keep seeking and keep knocking until that door opens. You know the answer is behind the door and you know who is behind that door; you just have to keep knocking until God opens it wide for you, and He will in Jesus Name.

God expects us to do things with a spirit of excellence, and to get to that level, sometimes, it may take a little while longer before we can operate on that next level; or the next spiritual realm, but we must not stop where we are. We must keep going, for the blessings of God are right around the corner.

KEY#4 – CONSISTENT

QUESTIONS – APPLICATION – REFLECTION –EXCEL'LE'RATION

C -Consistent – Luke 11:5-13

Q.A.R & E:

Q'S:

1. When you are consistent and persistent with God what happens?

_____.

2. What is the first thing you should do with the vision   you   have   been   given?

_____

A's:

2. What three things should we do to get results?

_____,

_____, _____.

3. If nothing is happening when you do those three things,   what   should   you   do?

_____.

R's:

4. What happens when we are relentless in the things of   God?

_____
.

5. How can you improve upon being consistent?
_____
_____.

E'S:

5. **What happens before we receiveth?** _____ .

6. **Findeth?** _____ .

7. **And before it's opened?** _____ .

What can you do spiritually to increase your rate of consistency? _____ .

Let Us Pray: _"Lord God, teach us wisdom on how we can better organize our lives, to give your name Glory, Amen."_

Let Us Pray: _"Lord please give us the tenacity to stay consistent & persistent with the daily, weekly challenges and tasks you have ordained for us to complete, for your glory In Jesus Name, Amen."_

M&M: Luke 11:10 - [10] For every one that asketh receiveth; and he that seeketh findeth, and to him that knocketh it shall be opened.

FOCUS KEY#5

U – UNITY

iF4LM Motto Text: 1 Cor. 13:1-13.

Unity & Love.

Unity is the state of being one. The state or fact of being united or combined into one, the oneness of mind, absence of diversity.

Unity is something that is critical to every individual in every walk of life. For instance, the couple who are raising their children up to be respectful to their parents must come to a common agreement on what it means to be respectful, or else the children can get mixed messages, resulting, at times, in children trying to manipulate their way into getting what they want.

In the school system, if there are no clearly defined boundaries on what is considered "bullying" when these types of issues come up and should be addressed, then many youths will continue to experience this same type of abuse on a regular basis.

Unity means the state of being joined together or in agreement.

Therefore, in the above examples of the meaning of the word Unity, it is important to be in agreement. This agreement is for any group of people or organization. We, the organization or group of people must first walk in peace to be successful; this will fortify (protect the group of people) with strength.

This same type "unity & love" should go on within the governments, countries and even in the world. If not, we will have what we call "war or warfare." Our country at this moment is in a great division, from racism to violence on many levels. Currently, other countries are about to be at war with us due to a lack of agreement and understanding. When a person feels that they can bully their way in controlling another country to do what they want them to do, that makes one angry and feeling cornered. What happens when one is feeling cornered is they come out fighting.

What is the answer? The answer has always been loving; mutual respect, not dictatorship nor brute force of power.

This love is often used in comparison to a relationship between a husband and a wife.

For a husband and wife to walk in love, a united front must be shown in order for peace to be sustained in the relationship. "In all your getting, get an understanding..." Proverbs 4:7

Ephesians 4:13 "Till we all come in the unity of the faith, and of the knowledge of the Son of God, unto a perfect man, unto the measure of the stature of the fullness of Christ:"

The importance of this unity is the "oneness." We can all be walking, talking, thinking and working together with that common bond – to make a change and build the Kingdom of God with full impact and effectiveness. There is strength in numbers, but there is power when everyone is forcefully advancing together.

You know, I have had people ask me why I treat certain people kindly after knowing that they have done wrong things to me underhandedly. I tell them because God has had mercy upon me. Then I think back at the Word whereby the disciples asked how many times shall I forgive the person that has done me wrong, and the answer was that we should forgive them 70 times 70. Matthew 18:22. WOW! That's a whole lot of times, like 4900 times. Now that doesn't mean that we allow someone to continue running over us and to do us wrong, but it does mean that we forgive them more times than we can count, so to speak. Love covers a multitude of sins, the Word says, so when we show love to those who have done us wrong we, in fact, cover their sin with forgiveness and the sins can no longer be seen due to the love we used to cover up their sins. In other words, love "the hell out of them."

Unity is one of the most powerful forces that one can have in their organization. Unity can help an organization to grow not just laterally or vertically, but inwardly. Inwardly involves the soul, empathy, character, wisdom. For instance, when there is Unity or Love in the camp and someone has difficulty in understanding a system, process or protocol, instead of being quick to judge, write up, or reprimand the individual if you are the boss, supervisor or leader, you take time to explain what you need and take additional care and repetition to make sure they understand what you need –especially if the person is really trying their best to understand and work with excellence. Another word for this is having compassion. If you or your organization or group lacks compassion, then it is time to do a reassessment of your true mission.

Lastly, love is able to cover all the faults, shortcomings, errors of not only others but also yourself. When you have unconditional love for others, God shows you unconditional love along with favor. So the next time you want to snap at someone, cuss them out, hit them, rebuke, fire, reprimand, ignore, etc., ask yourself, "did I show true love towards that person?" Let not your love be only because someone told you it should be this way, but allow your love to come from the heart, and if by any means you find it very difficult to love that person, others or group of people, then ask God to create within you a clean heart, to purge your heart from sin and iniquity. We may not want to admit it, but if we are always complaining and finding fault with others, perhaps the biggest issue is not other people or the group, but you; IT'S YOU. Simply repent and ask God to cleanse your heart and show you from this point forward how you can love others better. Selah.

TAKING Q.A.R.E. OF BUSINESS SECTION:

KEY#5 – UNITY

QUESTIONS – APPLICATION – REFLECTION –EXCEL'LE'RATION

U – UNITY – 1 Cor. 13:1-13

Q.A.R & E:

Q's:

1. Though I have the gift to speak in tongues and as an angel but don't have love, how do I sound? _____.

2. What am I if I know all prophecy, knowledge, faith, but no love? I am_____.

A's:

3. What if I give all to feed the poor and give my body as a sacrifice to burn, what happens? _____.

4. What is Charity/Love? List 5 Things
   1._____

_____ 3. _____ 4. _____ 5. _____ .

R's:

1. Which is the greatest between faith, hope, charity, sacrifice, humility?
   _____ .

2. How can you improve from the way you respond or treat others now?
   _____

E's:

1. What can you do now that will take your level of unity or love to another realm?
   _____

2. One scale of 1 to 10, how do you rate your love when working with others on your job_____, in your family_____ in ministry_____ in your business___.

FOCUS KEY#6

S - STRATEGY

iF4LM Motto Text: S - Strategy – Proverbs 24: 6-7, Joshua 6, I Chron.12:32,

The corporate strategy focuses on the organization as a whole, while the business unit strategy focuses on an individual business unit or market. Finally, team strategy identifies how a team will help the organization meet its overall goals and objectives. – Harvard Business School.

Strategy

6 For by wise guidance you can wage your war, And in an abundance of [wise] counselors there is victory and safety. Prov.24:6

It is wise to consult the minds of those whom you feel "have your best interest at heart" to give you some insight. They may not always have the answer, but perhaps they can guide your direction towards those who can, or at least attempt to give you some valuable information that could lead you in the right direction. In my personal journey of experiencing conflict or adversity, it is always better not to go through "it" alone. Firstly, we have to consult God. Secondly, ask advice from wise counsel. (More than likely, God has prepared them or made them ready through their own personal experience to give you the advice that would have you come out on top victorious). Often, what God has spoken to you will be confirmed through others. Sometimes your thoughts are so intense during those times of conflict that you need another head to give you sound judgment and to weigh things out.

7 Wisdom too exalted for a [hardened, arrogant] [a]fool; He does not open his mouth in the gate [where the city's rulers sit in judgment]. Proverbs 24:7

When wisdom comes to "a fool" he/she will reject it, and when that occurs, you just have to move on and leave them to their own devices.

Strategy is a method or plan chosen to bring about a desired future, such as the achievement of a goal or solution to a problem. – Wikipedia.

The vision God given to you is to bring forth fruit from the seed that had been planted within you. Trust in "the God" that is in you and that this God in you will take the gifts and bring them to pass. Start where you are; get your training, whether it by hands-on training, formal training, or Holy Ghost training.

Strategy (from Greek στρατηγία stratēgia, "art of troop leader; office of general, command, generalship"[1]) is a high-level plan to achieve one or more goals under conditions of uncertainty. In the sense of the "art of the general", which included several subsets of skills including "tactics", siegecraft, logistics, etc.

…Continued-Strategy-

The strategy is important because the resources available to achieve these goals are usually limited. Strategy generally involves setting goals, determining actions to achieve those goals, and mobilizing resources to execute the actions. A strategy describes how the ends (goals) will be achieved by the means (resources). – Wikipedia

In other words, when it comes to divine strategies, God will do things that look totally ridiculous, and at times don't make sense. The question is will you simply trust God, trust your feelings, or the natural mind? Being "Spirit-led" is the necessary key to walking in divine stratospheres.

"Then He answered and spake unto me, saying, This is the word of the LORD unto Zerubbabel, saying, Not by might, nor by power, but by my spirit, saith the LORD of hosts." Zechariah 4:6.

What I have also learned is to enjoy the process.

The word of God says, "Not that I speak from [any personal] need, for I have learned to be content [and self-sufficient through Christ, satisfied to the point where I am not disturbed or uneasy] regardless of my circumstances." Phil.4:11.

"Master what you already have, and then move on to the next task." When we are faithful over what the

Holy Spirit initially gives us, He will reward us, then give us something else to handle or implement. "His lord said unto him, well done, thou good and faithful servant: thou hast been faithful over a few things, I will make thee ruler over many things: enter thou into the joy of thy lord." Matthew 25:21

"The Holy Spirit is by far the greatest strategic tool God has given us to defeat any opposition and to advance the Kingdom of Heaven."

In conclusion, some of the greatest tools given to us to defeat the enemy and every evil and wicked device that comes against us are as follows:

#1 – the Holy Spirit, it's not by might nor by power, but by my spirit saith the Lord. Zechariah 4:6.

#2 – The Word of God, it is quicker and sharper than any two edged-sword. Hebrews 4:12.

#3 – Praise & Worship, "I will bless the Lord at all times His praise shall continually be in my mouth." Psalm 34:1.

#4 – Wisdom, "the fear of the Lord is the beginning of wisdom." "In all thy getting get an understanding." Proverbs 4:7

#5 – Love, the Love of God covers a multitude of sin. I Peter 4:8.

Let these five spiritual tools in life reign over your mind, body, soul, family, work, business, ministry and life,

– Apostle John W Rhodes

M&M: 1 Cor. 13:1-13

KEY#6 – STRATEGY

QUESTIONS – APPLICATION – REFLECTION –EXCEL'LE'RATION

S – STRATEGY – Proverbs 24:6-7, Joshua 6, I Chron.12:32

Q.A.R & E:

S - Strategy

Proverbs 24:6-7, Joshua 6, I Chron.12:32

Q's:

1. Strategy is the skillful use of a
   _____.

2. Strategy is a _____, _____, or series of_____ or stratagems for obtaining a _____ goal, _____ or objective.

3. What is in the multitude of counselors?
   _____.

A's:

1. How can I begin applying wise counsel properly? _____.

2. In Joshua 6, how many times did they compass the city? _____.

3. What can you do to increase your level of productivity using Divine Strategy_____.

4. Joshua in strategy_____ the people to do what in v.10_____.

R's:

1. The Wise and Foolish Builder: Matthew 7:24-27 - Jesus said a wise man who hears and does these sayings is like what? _____.

2. A Wise Builder does what before he builds? _____

3. According to Luke 14:28-30 The King Planning for Battle: Luke 14:31-32 The Unjust Steward: Luke 16:1-8

4. Faith without works is_____. This comes from what scripture? _____

5. What are five of the greatest spiritual tools given to us to defeat the enemy and every evil device that comes our way? _____ , _____ , _____ .

Let' Us Pray:

"Our Lord, King of Glory, patient in love, please grant us strength & wisdom to walk in your true love daily.

Teach us, and grant us your wisdom; even new ideas on how to be strategic and intentional in our daily planning.

Help us to be wise stewards of what you have given us, such as our time, gifts, talents, words, actions, resources, and abilities.

In these things, we ask, In Jesus Name, through you Our God.

M&M: Proverbs 24:6-7

"The Holy Spirit is by far the greatest strategic tool God has given us to defeat any opposition and to advance the Kingdom of Heaven."

In conclusion, some of the greatest tools given to us to defeat the enemy and every evil and wicked device that comes against us are as follows:

#1 – The Holy Spirit, "it's not by might nor by power, but by my spirit saith the Lord." Zechariah 4:6

#2 – The Word of God, "it is quicker and sharper than any two-edged sword." Hebrews 4:12

#3 – Praise & Worship, "I will bless the Lord at all times His praise shall continually be in my mouth." Psalm 32:1

#4 – Wisdom, "the fear of the Lord is the beginning of wisdom." "In all thy getting get an understanding." Proverbs 4:7

#5 – Faith, "Without Faith it is impossible to please God…" Hebrews 11:6

#6 – Works, "Faith without works is dead." Not legalistic works but works of action, after knowing what action the Holy Spirit has lead us to take. James 2: 14-26

#7 – Love, the Love of God covers a multitude of sin. I Peter 4:8.

Let these spiritual tools in life reign over your mind, body, soul, family, work, business, ministry and life,

– Apostle John W Rhodes.

It has been a great pleasure to share with you on how to Hit the Mark! It. In the spirit realm. My hopes are that you will use all that has been

shared with you in this book and go even beyond some of the simple, fundamental, powerful principles that will catapult you into your next level of success and calling.

We are so excited that to announce that even as you are reading this book, our next set of books/modules in this series are being written to help further your faith & spiritual development.

To continue on as "iFocus4Life Conqueror" to overcome the many obstacles which try to distract our progress or hinder our success due to lack of focus, join our iFOCUS4Life Conqueror Facebook Private Group. In addition, subscribe to Apostle John W Rhodes' Youtube Channel, BEEM YT Channel, http://beemtips.com to help you as a visionary and entrepreneur, and of course, go to http://johnwrhodes.com for other resources and upcoming materials. Get ready for our upcoming release: your New iFOCSU4Life Mastery Boot Camp and Course at http://ifocus4life.com

Until later remember, "When you focus your faith and pray, you are bound for an extraordinary destiny."

You are Victorious! John W Rhodes.

About the Author

John W. Rhodes grew up on the south side of Chicago, IL. , In a foster home. He is a graduate of Kentucky State University. John is an author of four books currently on amazon: WIT4Life, Bully Proof Nation, Bust the M.O.V.E.S., and Total Abundance. He has produced 2 Major CD's God's Call, and The Hand of God (available now on major online streaming services). John is the Founder & Senior Pastor of KOHA – Kingdom Of Heaven Assembly in Lexington, Ky.

www.kingdomofheavenassembly.org

You can find John W Rhodes' other resources at BLOG: www.johnwrhodes.com

Social Media Channels

FB: JohnWRhodes1

Twitter: JohnWRhodes1

Instagram: JohnWRhodes

Periscope: iFOCUSCOPE

Youtube Channel 1: ApostleJohnWRhodes

Youtube Channel 2: BEEM – Building Entrepreneurs with Elite Marketing